T0193431

A Virtuous Woman
"She's smart, strong, and she fears the Lord...
She rises at dawn and her lamp does not go out at night.
Her husband has total confidence in her and her
children rise up and call her blessed."
She shines bright for Jesus Christ!

P31W SHINE

The Journey to Becoming
a Proverbs 31 Woman

DR. TAMEKA TRASK

authorHOUSE®

AuthorHouse™
1663 Liberty Drive
Bloomington, IN 47403
www.authorhouse.com
Phone: 1 (800) 839-8640

Published by AuthorHouse 05/16/2019

ISBN: 978-1-7283-1260-6 (sc)
ISBN: 978-1-7283-1258-3 (hc)
ISBN: 978-1-7283-1259-0 (e)

Library of Congress Control Number: 2019942656

Contents

Introduction vii

Chapter 1: Rejected by Man, but Chosen by God 1

Chapter 2: Don't Fake it Until you Make it, Faith it Until
you Make it 9

Chapter 3: The Goal is to be Wise, not Perfect 17

Chapter 4: The Temptation that you're Fighting is
Nothing More than a Temporary Fix 25

Chapter 5: Discover your Purpose... Now Walk in it! 31

Poem: The Virtuous Woman of Proverbs 31 39

Chapter 6: Embrace the New you 45

Chapter 7: I was Chosen by God to be a Proverbs 31
Woman for my Husband 51

Chapter 8: P31W, it is Your Time to Shine 59

Conclusion 67

31 Daily I AM Affirmations 71

Poem: P31W Shine 75

My Prayer 79

Introduction

A Proverbs 31 Woman has always been a woman whom I've admired for years. She is the perfect example and model of a Godly woman. She gives us a clear picture of what a righteous woman, wife, and mother should strive to become. A Proverbs 31 Woman demonstrates superior work ethics and entrepreneurial skills. A Proverbs 31 Woman does not only describe married women but instead describes every virtuous woman. A virtuous woman is a woman both having and showing high moral standards. Once dissecting the 31st chapter of Proverbs 31, I began to learn the exact meaning behind it all. I then realized how truly attainable it was to become this Godly woman which the Bible speaks of. I came to the conclusion that it is a lifestyle, a behavior that I must adapt. A behavior that I had to allow to become not only a part of me but to become me entirely. This behavior wasn't something that I should practice turning on and off. It was more of a fixed behavior. It was a behavior which exemplified the woman I desired to be, and I was willing to become her at all costs. It was a must for me to be this woman in any given situation. I realized that in order to become her, I had to first change my mindset. I had to think like her, and then I would master becoming her. Once I realized that there was a certain mindset which I needed to obtain, I immediately developed a prayer life in order to win at becoming her. In 2012, during an encounter with the Lord, the Holy Spirit gave me a vision. I was shown a ministry of women! There were so many women that there was no way to number them. The women which I was shown appeared to be from diverse nationalities. Women from all over the world shining for Jesus in every area of their lives! The Holy Spirit spoke and informed me that I would be empowered by the Spirit of God to sharpen these women. It was made very clear that I would be using the word of God along with the power of God to accomplish this assignment. These women would then use the tools given to them to sharpen other women, causing a "Domino effect" and procreate true Proverbs 31 women throughout the world. These women will become better wives, mothers, and over-all women of God. Each woman would receive whatever God holds in store for her and live the life which God ordained for her to live. Winning her entire household for the kingdom of God would be both her main priority and ultimate outcome. This will be covered more in-depth later.

Chapter 1

REJECTED BY MAN, BUT CHOSEN BY GOD

As a child, I knew that there was something different that I possed on the inside of me. It was something that I didn't understand. Something unique and supernatural. The young me couldn't explain or even comprehend it all. There was so much which I was able to see in the spiritual realm. At times, I was also able to hear the Holy Spirit speak to me. At the age of eleven, I finally stopped sleeping with my parents. Due to nightmares and prophetic dreams, I found myself unable to sleep alone. I would wake up in the middle of the night screaming for help constantly. My mother would always comfort me, and sometimes my father. I never witnessed my siblings or cousins having these experiences. I would see spiders, cockroaches, and snakes. It was indeed terrifying for a little kid! There is one moment in particular which I can recall vividly. I was only at eleven years of age, and I had a cousin whom I loved dearly. She wasn't my blood relative, but we called one another cousins since she and my blood cousin were best friends (with all due respect, I will keep her identity concealed). I looked up to her being that she was the most beautiful, popular, and loved individual that I knew at the time. She loved her some me and would light up like a Christmas tree each time she saw me. She was about eight or nine years older than I. Undoubtedly, I admired her and wanted to follow in her footsteps. When she came around I felt the love and never felt rejected. She would hug me and kiss me every time she greeted me. I could still remember her smile, and it was one of a kind. I will never forget the way she called my name in her loud boisterous tone. She would call out to me saying, "Hey Meeeekaaa!" A huge smile present on her face. This suddenly became a permanent memory. One weekend when she stopped by my mother's house for a visit, she was only there for a little while and when it came time for her to leave someone gave her a ride. I walked with her outside and she proceeded to sit in the backseat of the car. She was looking directly at me from the back window. She exclaimed, "Bye Meeeekaaa!" and smiled extremely wide. I returned a goodbye to her, but she never stopped waving and smiling until the car became out of my view (tears are falling as I write this). I waved and instantly heard the Holy Spirit speak to me saying, "You will never forget her goodbye." I did mention her prolonged waving to other family members who were around, but everyone laughed it off. Still, for some unknown reason, I couldn't get the image out of my head. Unfortunately, a few days later she was murdered… God was revealing my prophetic gift to me at the age of eleven, but I was too inexperienced to recognize the calling on my life. I was extremely hurt and couldn't keep myself together. I was very angry because she was someone whom I believed would be around for a long time. Singing and music became therapeutic for me. However, church and God's word was my true joy. I had, and still have to this day, such a genuine love for the Lord as well as a burning desire to serve Him. At the tender age of five, I was baptized at "Bible Way Missionary Baptist" church, a small church located in New Orleans, Louisiana. The church was my entire life. My mother was what some people would consider being a "Holy Rolly". She loved the Lord and was known for her powerful prayer life, along with her knowledge of God's word. My mother knew the Bible from front to back! Being that there are seven days in a week, we went to church at least five days out of those seven. Not to mention that on Sundays it was an all-day affair from sun-up to sun-down. My siblings and cousins would murmur and complain at times, but not me! I was always eager and ready with a huge smile on my face because I was going to church. My mother loved every bit of it. When I was really little, I was apart of the "Sunshine Children's" choir at our church. For rehearsal, I could recall begging to sing lead and was never chosen or even given a chance. It wasn't a good feeling at all. I actually felt what it was like to be heartbroken at five years old. I can remember crying out to my mother, "Why aren't they choosing me?!" I mentioned to her that I knew I could do it and would be great at it. As time went on, rehearsal after rehearsal passed and I still wasn't chosen to sing lead. I could remember thinking to myself, "I will show everyone that I can do it." On the following Sunday when it came time to sing, I stepped up from the rest of the kids and sung loud as can be without missing a beat! The entire church was smiling, laughing, and clapping. I knew that God was real, and He wanted me to do just what I had done. He wanted me to be bold for Jesus! I've been bold ever since. It's not that people don't see the greatness in you, they just refuse to acknowledge your brightness in fear of you outshining them or those which they would rather shine the brightest. A lot of people don't want you to know that they actually see greatness exist on the inside of you, so they tend to ignore or reject your gifts. They would much rather keep you in doubt and stop you from believing in yourself. Some people don't want you to realize that you are great and that your greatness is definitely noticed by others. They fear that if they tell you that you're great, you will begin to believe in yourself. Once a person believes in themselves, they will discover who and what they were destined to become. Once a person discovers who they are, no level of rejection will matter to them. They will then be aware that they hold the key to their own success. Often times people fear the possibility of you reaching a higher level than where they are in their lives. What people fail to realize is that we all have greatness on the inside of us. Praying to God and developing a closer relationship with him will allow anyone to discover who they truly are. God will expose to you your true purpose, but you must spend quality time with Him daily. Once you discover your purpose, Satan will know that it's all over for him. There will be no limit in you because there is no limit in your God. It's clear why Satan uses the spirit of rejection to get you off track and feeling helpless, hopeless, and unworthy of becoming great in life. He uses other people to accomplish this feeling of despair. You must realize that you hold on the inside of you everything that you'll ever need to be great in this life. God has already ordained you to be all that He has chosen you to be. Scripture has it in Jeremiah 1:5- "Before I formed thee in the belly I knew thee, and before thou camest forth out of the womb I sanctified thee and I ordained thee a prophet unto the nations." This scripture gives me life because no matter the rejection of man, God will still carry out His perfect plan for your life. Your life has been ordained by God from the very beginning. From my perspective, the spirit of rejection is somewhat of a monster trying to frighten you away from your purpose. The enemy uses the spirit of rejection at an attempt to discourage you from believing in yourself. I speak liberty to everyone who is reading my book and is currently under the spell of rejection. You won't be held back any longer in the mighty name of Jesus Christ! The spirit of the Lord has come to set you free. You have greatness on the inside of you and you shall do great things in God's kingdom. Now let's take a moment to reflect on the word rejection. To reject is to refuse, decline, turn down, to forsake, and to totally abandon someone or something. After reading this, the first thing which comes to my mind is, "To reject someone is to deny them of their opportunity to present to you the greatness which they possess inside." There are many different levels of rejection in my opinion, the greatest being the act of abortion. I am completely against abortions because it's technically a form of robbery. You're taking away a human being's chance to fulfill their life's purpose. If the mother of the president of the United States would have aborted him, then he would've never become president. That was only an example, but you get the point. If Jeremiah 1:5 states, "Before God formed you in the belly He knew you...", that literally means that every aborted baby was known by God before the moment of conception. Because of the influence of Satan for whatever reason, that soul was rejected before ever living. People, before you existed in this natural world which we see with our natural eyes, our existence was already in the supernatural. The supernatural is simply the spiritual world which we cannot see with our natural eyes. So yes, before the conception of that baby God already knows the individual. Before a visual appearance of a baby by what's known to be an ultrasound, God saw that baby and knew them according to scripture. Don't allow anyone to tell you that you were and are a mistake. You were indeed formulated by God on purpose. No matter how many times you have failed in life, you are somebody. Just because you've failed, it doesn't mean you are a failure. There is no reason on the face of this earth good enough to make you feel that you don't have greatness on the inside of you. There is no mistake which you have made in your life bad enough to make you feel as though you are nothing, or that you don't have greatness on the inside of you. Nothing can stop the plan of God for your life. Whoever rejected you, that's their loss and not your concern. You are somebody and that somebody in you is great. God loves you and He is a forgiving God. He sent His son Jesus Christ to die on the cross for all of your sins, mistakes, and imperfections. It is time for you to rise and shine and to believe in yourself. Now is the time for you to become all that God has chosen you to be in this life. Don't allow the spirit of rejection to keep you bound any longer. I am a living witness of someone who has been rejected by man countless times, but I have been chosen by God.

I choose to rise above that rejection and shine bright like the diamond that I am. I declare that millions of women will take a stand with me and show Satan that we are free from the spirit of rejection. Together we can show that we won't be held down any longer! Let's make a difference in the world. Take a vow and don't stop until you reach your destiny. When you feel you've reached your destiny, then aim higher. God has a perfect plan for your life! No matter who has rejected you, remember that God has chosen you.

Chapter 2

DON'T FAKE IT UNTIL YOU MAKE IT, FAITH IT UNTIL YOU MAKE IT

What is faith? Scripture has it in Hebrews 11:1- "Now faith is the substance of things hoped for the evidence of things not seen…" Before we go any further, I want you to think of faith as a spirit. That's right, faith is a spiritual force! This spiritual force is alive and is working at this present moment and time. That is why Hebrews 11:1 starts off by stating "NOW FAITH!" After meditating on that scripture, I instantly realized that I must operate in faith every second of the day. Faith isn't a "use it then lose it until you need it again" type of force. Not at all. There is no way that I, or anyone for that matter, can use the same faith which we used one year ago. You aren't even able to use the same faith which you used yesterday for today! Faith is a spiritual force which lives and works in this very second. A Proverbs 31 woman needs to always operate in her NOW FAITH in order to be a victor in every area of her life and not a victim. Satan would love for us to be victims, and that is why he's always fighting our progress. He wants us to lose hope. You must never lose hope! "Faith is the substance of things hoped for and the evidence of things not seen." Instead we must fight the good fight of faith against all of the fiery darts of the evil one. Each time Satan attacks you by firing those evil darts, you must use the faith which God has given you to both combat and overcome those evil attacks. Some common examples of fiery darts would be the attacks against your health or against your finances. When Satan comes to attack marriages and relationships, these are also forms of fiery darts. He doesn't fight fair. He will even come against your children, which is another fiery dart. He attacks individuals on their jobs. When people hate on you for no reason whatsoever, that is also considered a fiery dart. I could go on and on, however we must stand strong on God's holy word, believing that God means every word that he says in the Bible. We must fight until our victory has been won! So many women believe in faking it until they make it, but the reality is this… There is only so much faking that you can do. I would advise you to get serious about your faith walk. Faking that your faith is great won't defeat Satan, nor will it defeat his tricks. The devil wants your faith to be weak. He wants you to fake your level of faith, or fake the fact that you are even operating in faith at all. The enemy knows that if you don't use your level of faith which God has given unto you, you'll then be giving him the ammunition to be able to shoot more of his fiery darts your way. Not only will he shoot, but he'll ultimately destroy you and your loved ones. It is time to take a stand and show the devil once and for all that he is fighting a losing battle. You shall arise and become the woman of faith which God has chosen you to be. The gift of faith is rightfully yours! Faith is a free gift given by God which is a great weapon that is needed in the event of spiritual warfare. Scripture has it in 2 Corinthians 10:4- "For the weapons of our warfare are not carnal but mighty through God to the pulling down of strong holds…" So you see, we definitely need spiritual weapons to defeat and destroy the evil one. We only need to use the spiritual weapons which God gives us. Remember the saying "You can't bring a knife to a gunfight"? Well, you can't bring natural physical weapons to a spiritual fight either. God has given each one of us a measure of faith. You can find that scripture in Romans 12:3. Your faith may not be in the same measure as my faith, but we each have been given faith through God's grace. In order for your faith to work, you must exercise it by using it without ceasing. I have been a woman of faith for as long as I can remember. Faith was all that I had to get me through the most difficult and trying times of my life. Ladies, in order to become successful on your journey in blossoming into that Proverbs 31 woman, walking in faith will have to be one of your main priorities. Your mission in life should be to please God. Hebrews 11:6 tells us that, "Without faith it is impossible to please God…" You must operate in faith on purpose. Once you get an understanding of the spirit of faith, and do whatever is necessary to ensure that you are living a life of faith, everything will begin to fall into place. You need to have an attitude as, "I am not where I want to be, but I thank God that I am not where I used to be. I will continue working on getting to the place which God wants me to be. I will soon reach that place of destiny through faith." God has generously given you everything that you need in order to become a Proverbs 31 woman. Becoming a Proverbs 31 woman is not an overnight accomplishment, however it IS a forever lifestyle. Did you know that everything you've gone through in life and everything that has caused you pain, both the trials and tribulations you've faced, God is actually using those experiences to bring out the best in you. He's using those experiences to mold you and shape you into becoming a Proverbs 31 woman. You must faith it until you make it on your journey to becoming this Godly woman.

Anything that you do in life will require faith. You won't even be able to accomplish even the smallest task in life without having faith. You must also understand that you have to put in the work in order to become the woman that you desire to be in life. James 2:17 tells us that- "Faith without works is dead…" Having faith is like having an empty garden. Once you decide that you want to grow your faith, you must plant seeds. Think about it, what's the sense in growing a garden if you don't intend to have beautiful plants and flowers. That is the exact same way you must think of faith. God has given you faith, but what's the sense of having that measure of faith if you are not going to use it? The number one way to increase and build your faith is with the word of God. The word of God is what you need to use in order to plant the seeds in your garden of faith. When you read, study, meditate, and quote scriptures, you are actually growing your faith. The seeds which you plant today will determine how great your harvest of faith will be tomorrow. You mustn't stop there because now it is time to take the next step to seeing the results of operating in faith. It is time to put some action behind your faith! After you've planted the seeds within your garden of faith by meditating on God's word, quoting scriptures, and studying, the next step is to be a doer of God's word. Scripture has it in James 1:22- "But be ye doers of the word and not hearers only..." The Bible is confirming that it is very important for us to take what we've read and apply it to our lives. If not, your faith will grow stagnant. You must use that measure of faith which God gives to each one of us and build it up by becoming a doer of God's word. I can remember when I was seventeen years old and needed to pass the LEAP exam. The LEAP was the exit exam which we were required to pass in order to graduate from high school. I failed the science portion twice and I knew that I had to do something fast. As a method of preparation, I read my word, prayed, and attended tutoring sessions regularly. Mind you, I was approaching my third and final time to attempt the science portion of the exit exam. This was my first recollection of my faith being tested, however my faith was great. I knew that I was going to pass. In the end, I passed my LEAP test and was qualified to graduate with my senior class. God is so good and faith works, but only if you work it. So much has transpired over the years since then but every time a situation arises, I just think of God's goodness and how he made a way for me previously. Can you imagine how much my faith has grown over the years due to all of the many seeds which I've planted in my garden of faith? I will never doubt God, for he has been beyond good to me. We must realize that our faith will not move ahead of us. The spirit of faith will not move unless you move first. You are the master of your own faith. The spirit of faith in your life will only do what you allow it to do. You are in control of how your measure of faith will work in your favor. Some people have victory in areas where others seem to be defeated in. Most of the time it's because those individuals who weren't defeated worked their measure of faith. Work your faith, and in return witness your faith work for you. Faith is indeed my life. I sincerely walk by faith and not by sight. That is what 2 Corinthians 5:7 tells us to do. Habakkuk 2:4 states that, 'The just shall live by faith..." The just meaning "righteous".

It took faith for us to be saved and become the children of God in the first place. You must be willing to do whatever it takes to grow your faith which already exists. A Proverbs 31 woman cannot under any circumstances fake her faith. If she so happens to do so, she will be exposed when tough situations arise in her life. The "fake it until you make it" mentality will get you nowhere in life. On the other hand, the "faith it until you make it" mentality will open up doors which no man can shut. As Proverbs 31 women, we need mountain moving faith. I'm referring to the level of faith that will certainly set us apart from the rest. It is time for you to start operating in your faith the way God designed for you to. I want to encourage you to start exercising your faith today. If you follow these instructions, your life will never be the same in Jesus name! Hang in there, you are getting closer to becoming the Proverbs 31 woman which the Bible speaks of. Get ready because this is your season!

Chapter 3

The Goal is to be Wise, not Perfect

So many women struggle everyday trying to be this perfect individual, but that "perfect woman" clearly only exist in fictional stories. Ladies, I need you to read this upcoming statement as many times necessary in order for it to register. There is ABSOLUTELY NO PERFECT WOMAN IN THIS WORLD. We all have flaws! If you are pressuring yourself daily to become this perfect person, then you might as well give up now. Perfection should never be the goal of a Proverbs 31 woman. It is impossible to become perfect because we all mess up at times. God understands that perfection is totally out of our grasp as human beings. For instance, If we were perfect then there would be no need for God. God uses our imperfections in order to draw us closer to him. We as imperfect individuals will always need a perfect God. Imagine being a trophy wife, a perfect mom and friend, a perfect family member, as well as a perfect business woman. What if life on earth had absolutely no hate? Simply a life with only admiration and love. What if nothing ever went wrong in our lives ever? Okay, now let's get back to reality because that type of life is absolutely nonexistent. The world which we live in is too chaotic and imperfect for that.

,

With that being said, the people living in the word could never be perfect. A Proverbs 31 Woman is simply a woman who has committed herself to Jesus Christ. She's a woman who loves God and her family. A woman who's willing to do whatever it takes to make sure that her home is in perfect harmony. When we accept Jesus as Lord and Savior of our lives, while also following his footsteps, it produces change in every area of our lives. As you continue on your journey to becoming a Proverbs 31 woman, you will learn that wisdom is a necessity, not an option. Scripture has it in Proverbs 4:7 that, "Wisdom is the principal thing..." Having wisdom allows you to commit to the things of God. Wisdom also ushers in a spirit of obedience to Christ. When an individual allows wisdom to lead them, they will find themselves making better decisions in life for themselves as well as their families. A wise person will always choose good over evil and right over wrong. As you grow and develop, the gift of wisdom will also grow and develop within you. Making wiser choices in life is a true behavior of a mature individual. Wisdom will soon become apart of a mature Christian. As a Proverbs 31 woman, wife, and mother, it's essential to build your home on a foundation of wisdom. Proverbs 24:3 states, "Through wisdom is a house built and by understanding it is established." A wise woman is led by the Holy Spirit, and she will have it no other way. When a woman seeks to be perfect, she limits herself from being a great wife, mother, and Godly woman. Seeking to be perfect in life will only frustrate you. It is impossible to operate at your greatest level of potential with a spirit of frustration. The key to developing your greatness is discovering your strengths, as well as your weaknesses. A Proverbs 31 woman knows what her strengths are and magnifies them all while minimizing her weaknesses only to revisit them at the appropriate time. Once you discover what your strengths are, then at that point your building process will become more promising. The goal is to become better in the areas which you fall short in all while mastering the areas which you are strong in. One of the reasons why many women fail at becoming better in their gifted areas is because they're too busy coveting what another woman already has. Be confident in who God made you to be without competing with other women and desiring another woman's position in life. Comparing yourself to other women will distract you from your ultimate goal. If you aren't looking in another woman's direction to help make her better, or to be inspired, then you shouldn't be looking in her direction to compete. A woman whose goal is to be wise is aware of the fact that unhealthy competition isn't a form of wisdom. A wise woman desires to be only who God has chosen her to be. An original will always have a more authentic shine than a copy. Making this type of mistake on your journey to becoming a Proverbs 31 woman can be very detrimental. Instead work on building your confidence so that you can shine brightest in your own way. As you move along on your journey to becoming a Proverbs 31 woman, remember that there is a difference between meekness and weakness. Be sure not to get those two confused. Also keep in mind that it's better to have a heart of humbleness opposed to a heart of haughtiness. Additionally, a Proverbs 31 woman knows the importance of correction. However, she corrects with love and she doesn't want to ever operate in a spirit of hate. She knows the importance of order, so she never conducts herself in a disorderly fashion. As a Proverbs 31 woman you must be cautious of the words which exit your mouth. Your words are powerful and once spoken they could never be taken back. A wise woman would rather use her words to speak life and she uses her words to build her house. She'll never use her words to bring destruction, ultimately tearing her house down. Proverbs 14:1 states, "Every wise woman buildeth her house: but the foolish plucketh it down with her hands…" Your words create your atmosphere. Speak blessings over your children, husband, and all things pertaining to your life. You must program yourself with God's word in order to never speak words of doom, but instead words of life. Some of you don't see the life you desire because you don't speak the life that you desire. Whenever you have a disagreement with your husband, you must remember that you can't always have the last word or try to prove that you are right all the time. Peace should be more important than proving a point. As a Proverbs 31 woman, the peace and harmony of your home should never be compromised.

I can count on one hand how many times my husband and I have had an argument in ten years! This is because I've learned that it's not always beneficial to give an answer. All battles should be chosen wisely. Answers which are unspoken are sometimes the most powerful answers. Silence never killed anyone, however speaking unnecessarily can definitely kill your marriage. Scripture has it in Proverbs 21:19 that, "It is better to live in a desert than in a house with a quarrelsome woman…"

Ladies, be your man's peace. Remember that he's constantly fighting spiritual battles on a day to day basis. It is a fight just to get home in one piece as a man in the times that we are living in. You must live a self controlled life as a Proverbs 31 woman. You must not allow your emotions to control your behavior, instead get in control of your emotions so that your behavior can exemplify a true woman of God. Satan loves to attack us emotionally. He knows that when we are emotionally unstable, we aren't capable of making wise decisions. The devil knows exactly what buttons to push in order to get us bent out of shape and off of track. Before you know it, your mind isn't in the right place, which causes you to be unable to think clearly. It is extremely important ladies as Godly women for us to emulate a woman of noble character. Living as a woman which Christ wants you to live as will make your father God in Heaven so happy. Psalms 37:4 states, "Delight yourself in the Lord and he will give you the desires of your heart. To delight in something is to simply be happy regarding that matter. Try it! Try making

God happy and witness Him move in your life like never before. Everything that your heart desires, God will grant it unto you because he delights in your ways. Whatever the word of God says, that settles it. I'm going in the direction of God's word. What about you? Some of you may be thinking that this P31W life is not for you because maybe you fear that you'll never make it far in your journey. If you can relate and you're struggling in this area, don't lose heart. Simply begin to pray to God and ask Him to help you in the areas which you are weak in. He will definitely answer your prayers. It's so important to read your Bible and surround yourself with positive women who are headed in the same direction as you are. "Iron sharpens iron so one man sharpens the countenance of his friend." - Proverbs 27:17. We all are a work in progress and no one has arrived. Don't get frustrated, instead be empowered remember, it is not about perfection. It's about becoming wise in our decision making. As a Proverbs 31 woman, there is no time to make unwise decisions. You're going somewhere! You have a destiny to reach! Wasted time could never be replaced. Your family is counting on you to be able to make wise decisions. In order to help lead them in the right direction. The gift of wisdom would allow a mother to discern when her children are in the presence of bad company. A wise wife knows how to keep her husband from falling into a trap that the enemy set up for his demise.

A wise woman knows how to take care of her home without neglecting self care. Remember, it's not about being a perfect woman living a perfect life. It's more so about becoming a wise woman living a life of enjoyment all while serving God. You too can begin this life today! Start by confessing the exact life that you want for you and your family. Here are some of the golden rules! You must learn to speak it and believe it and you will witness the manifestation of it. It is time for you to believe in yourself! You're more than what the enemy wants you to see yourself as. Scripture has it in Romans 8:37 that, "You are more than a conqueror." Now push through, keep the main goal before you, and do what's necessary to reach your other goals. The main goal is to be a wise woman, not a perfect woman. You are well on your way to becoming the Proverbs 31 woman that the Bible speaks of in Proverbs chapter 31. Get ready to experience life on another level. I speak prophetically that a shift has now taken place in your life!

Chapter 4

THE TEMPTATION THAT YOU'RE FIGHTING IS NOTHING MORE THAN A TEMPORARY FIX

Oh, how awesome! You're moving along so wonderfully on your journey to becoming a brand new woman. You will soon become that Proverbs 31 woman which the Bible speaks of, but you must keep in mind that everyone won't be happy for you. The devil himself despises this new and improved woman you are becoming. If he had it his way, he would have hindered you a long time ago. This is the stage in your journey where people are noticing your transformation. Satan will use whatever and whoever he can to disrupt your progress. Scripture has it in John 10:10 that, "The thief (the devil) comes only to steal, kill and destroy. I, Jesus, came that they may have life and have it more abundantly…" You must pray for and have a spirit of discernment during your transformation period in order to judge effectively. Without the ability to judge correctly, you become a victim of the enemy's attacks. Because the devil hates it when the people of God progress, he plots against you even the more each time you progress. You must analyze everything that presents itself to you in order to receive the clarification which you need to make the proper judgement in any given situation. I personally ask myself two questions before making a final decision regarding anything. Number one, "Is this going to help me receive the abundant life that Jesus wants me to have?", or "Is this going to give Satan the ability to steal, kill, and possibly destroy me?" When you learn to narrow down your decision making process to those two options, you will come to realize how much easier it is to eliminate whatever serves you no purpose. You must come to the realization that Satan is a skillful and cunning force. He's been studying you from the very beginning. As a child, the devil watched you closely. He's aware of your likes, your dislikes and your gifts, but most importantly he's aware of your weaknesses. The areas which you fall short in are no secret to him, which is why you have struggled for years to overcome your weaknesses. The devil has tempt you time and time again in the area he knows your strength is challenged. Why? He wants you to give up, he would rather you to throw in the towel. You MUST fight temptation, it's ONLY a temporary fix. Training yourself to resist temptation on every level will be beneficial throughout your journey. Scripture has it in James 4:7,

"Submit yourselves therefore to God. Resist the devil, and he will flee from you." A Proverbs 31 woman knows the importance of submission. When we submit to God, He is then able to give us the willpower which we're going to need to fight all temptation. Speaking of submission, here's something to think about. How can any women properly submit to their husbands if they haven't yet submitted to their heavenly father, God? Scripture has it in Ephesians 5:22, "Wives, submit yourselves unto your own husbands as unto the Lord..." So as you can see it states "as unto the Lord", meaning that your ability to properly submit to your husbands comes after properly submitting yourselves unto God first. Once you've followed the instruction given in God's word, there will be no temptation on the face of this earth that you won't be woman enough to fight off. You must become an expert in fighting the temptations of life because you are at war with a very artful enemy, and he doesn't play fair. That is exactly why when trouble arises, and you hit the lowest point in your life, what the enemy does is present temptation to you as an antidote. Still, you must keep in mind that it is only a temporary fix appearing to be a permanent cure to whatever problem you are faced with. When you are at your lowest point in life, your discernment is sometimes off.

That's why it's necessary to develop a prayer life, for then you can request that the Holy Spirit helps you as you fight off the temptation. Here's an example of a short and straight to the point prayer that you may use… "Dear God, I need you now. Holy Spirit, help me to fight off this temptation which I am currently faced with. The blood of Jesus Christ has given me the power to stand against the attacks of the enemy. I will not yield to any temptation. Thank you father God for giving me the strength to win this war. In Jesus Christ name, Amen." This prayer is certainly short, but it's powerful and it works! Keep in mind that every temporary fix appears real, but it's not the real deal. It is counterfeit! Just like counterfeit money, it looks real and it feels real, but it's not. As a young lady working in retail, I was taught to hold large bills up to the light in order to see if it's real or fake. Well, the same thing applies to every situation we're faced with in our lives. Bring everything to God in prayer and the light of God, which is the Spirit of God, will illuminate the situation and give you clarity. As a Proverbs 31 woman, you are never to search, nor settle, for temporary fixes. You should only be receptive to that which is genuine, significant, and long lasting in life. Anything outside of those three requirements could very well be fraudulent, irrelevant, and will last for a limited time only. Scripture has it in 1 Corinthians 10:13, "There hath no temptation taken you but such as is common to man: but God is faithful, Who will not suffer you to be tempted above that ye are able; but will with the temptation also make a way to escape, that ye may be able to bare it. I don't know about you, but every time I read that scripture I shout, "Hallelujah! Glory to God!" Ladies, that scripture is simply stating that God has given us the power which we need to fight off temptation. God has provided a way of escape for each of His children. Thank you, Jesus! We have the victory so don't you dare believe Satan's lies any longer. You are not the defeated one and you don't have to yield unto temptation. That is why we must learn scripture and study the word of God to show ourselves approved, according to 2 Timothy 2:15. When you don't know the word, the devil uses that against you. The devil will have you thinking that falling into the trap of any temptation is just apart of life, but that is not true and certainly not the way of living the life of a Proverbs 31 woman. Now the reality is this... we will always be tempted. That is simply apart of life, however being tempted is not a sin. Jesus himself was tempted according to Matthew 4:1-11. With that being said, it should come as no surprise that we will be tempted as well. We must refuse every temptation which comes our way. Once we refuse the temptation, Satan has no legal right to infiltrate what belongs to the targeted individual. Just to clarify, this doesn't mean that he won't return or try to tempt you again. That is why you must continue to fight any temptation and win over your weaknesses. Although weaknesses are present in your life, you don't have to succumb to those weak areas. Get in control of the choices you make and never allow the enemy to gain control of you. When the enemy has control over an individual, it paralyzes their abilities to make the right decisions. If there is anything that should stick with you after reading this chapter, remember this... Learn to acknowledge your weaknesses, but most importantly take them to God in prayer. If you so happen to make a mistake, don't get comfortable in your error. Don't make plans to do better, take action to do better. A plan may never take place, but taking action will replace a failed plan and produce incredible results. Continue reading for you are gaining the personal and spiritual development in order to become the Proverbs 31 woman which the Bible speaks of.

Chapter 5

DISCOVER YOUR PURPOSE...
NOW WALK IN IT!

In order to discover your purpose, you must first identify your passion. Your passion holds the key to your treasure, however your treasure can only be unlocked as you begin to walk in your divine purpose. If you don't have a strong attraction, excitement, and/or enthusiasm for whatever you're doing, you more than likely haven't discovered your true passion in life. You must be true to yourself. Here's a little activity which will help you work towards fulfilling the goal of discovering your true purpose. First off, write down everything that you lack interest in doing. For example, some people may not enjoy teaching, so they'd write that down on their paper. Once you have completed that list, then you must write the things which you are okay with doing. For example, it's something that you could tolerate doing and won't mind doing, but it doesn't move your spirit man. As a reference, your "spirit man" is the powerful force on the inside of you which often steers you in the right direction. Many would describe it in a way of saying,

"Something inside of me said…", but realize that this is the Spirit of God which lives on the inside of you.

Ok let's get back to the activity, once you've written those things down, you'll realize how much time you've wasted working in those fields and areas which God never intended for you to work in. Now here's the appropriate way to discover your purpose in life… You must begin by seeking God through prayer for direction. Once you've sought God, write down everything you're truly passionate about. These would be the endeavors which move your spirit man in such a way as to bring total fulfillment to your life. Remember that your true purpose will always correlate with the things which you're passionate about. Scripture has it in Matthew 6:33, "But seek ye first the kingdom of God and his righteousness; and all of these things shall be added unto you…" Whenever you seek God for guidance, He will show you the way to go. When you put God and His kingdom work first, He will lead you to your God given purpose, which will ultimately lead you to your God given destiny. Right now, I want you to stop reading for a moment and put your thinking caps on. Now take a deep breath and think back to when you were a child. What was it that you enjoyed doing? Close your eyes and think about it for a moment. Personally, I can recall as a child loving to play church with my cousins… and of course I'm sure you could guess who the pastor was *laughs*. I could recall dressing up in my mother's clothes and shoes and styling hair. I also enjoyed pretending to be a teacher while teaching my dolls. I can remember teaching and preaching to an empty room filled with invisible people. I saw myself as a business woman at a very young age, visualizing myself owning my own businesses. As a matter of fact, in Junior High I would charge five dollars to style my school mate's hair. I'd also sell snacks at school to all of the students. See how my pastoral, and entrepreneurial skills existed inside of me from a young age? I am a pastor and an entrepreneur/business woman today! I love being a pastor and an entrepreneur, for it is my true purpose and passion! So you see, everything that I enjoyed doing as a little kid, I am living it now. Whatever captures your attention, move in that direction. What is it that interests you? As you unlock these things, you will be on your way to discovering your true purpose in life. Here are some things to keep in mind as you search for your true passion in order to discover your divine purpose. When you are passionate about something, you'll always contemplate new ideas and ways that you can nurture that passion. Even engaging in a conversation about your passion ignites a fire within you! Often times you'll realize that your passion will make you very emotional. You may even cry at times, especially when you're able to witness the positive long lasting effect that it has on others. When you are passionate about something, you will travel both near and far no matter the distance. Distance will never be able to keep you from your true passion. Also, when you are passionate about something, you aren't in it solely for the income but rather the outcome. Your passion has the power to ignite a fire in you like nothing else. This fire is neither replaceable, nor revocable. That's why it's very important not to confuse your interest with your passion. Your interests can change from one season to the next, but your passion is what sets your soul on fire. It makes every negative situation in the world seem minute, meaning small.

Irrelevant things, people, and situations won't be able to steal your attention. You will begin to protect your energy and your personal space. Why? Because when you are in the element you're meant to be in, you won't allow anyone or anything to cause you to lose your focus. Losing your focus will only take you back to that place of uncertainty. Being uncertain about your purpose in life will never be a joyous position. Now that you've discovered your true passion, your newfound passion will allow you to discover your divine purpose. Discovering your divine purpose in life is one of the best feelings in the entire world. This feeling is like no other! You've now learned something about yourself that's going to help give you the joy in life that you were only able to dream of. You didn't arrive to this place in life by your doing alone, nor anyone else's. You must realize that it was only the grace of God that allowed you to discover your purpose in life. It is time to get serious about walking in your purpose. As a Proverbs 31 woman, remember you are a life changer. Now that you've found your true purpose, you will always be on an assignment to help change the lives of others as well as cultivate and mentor them. Your purpose will always promote change for others. This stage of the journey is extremely important. You must keep your purpose before you always in order to remain purpose driven. No matter the problems or situations which may arise in your life. You must not allow it to interfere with the call that God has on your life. When you're driven by your purpose, you will never allow anything to stand in the way of you walking in your purpose. You will always be aware that your purpose comes from God and not man. It wasn't something that you magically received, but instead something that you received from God to help make the world a better place. Scripture has it in James 1:17, "Every good gift and every perfect gift is from above and cometh down from the Father of lights…" God is so amazing that He allows his light to shine in us and through us. The mindset of a Proverbs 31 woman is to always make an impact. She is never a selfish individual but a blessed individual. She loves to be a blessing to others by becoming a living example and being a servant in the kingdom of God. You must understand that everything you do from this point on will be greater than you. Every decision that you make from here on out will either demoralize you or invigorate you. At this stage in your journey, you will definitely need positive people around you. You need people in your life who believe in you and genuinely want to see you win. These people will not only witness you win, but help you work toward reaching your goals. The only way to stay purpose driven is to keep all unnecessary things and people out of your midst. You are well on your way to becoming the Proverbs 31 woman that the Bible speaks of. In this season God will do a lot of exposing, so don't be surprised if you find out that close family members and friends suddenly don't have your best interest at heart. Thank God for the exposure because elevation often requires separation. Don't allow the exposure process to slow you down because you MUST keep going. Keep your goal before you at all times. Once you reach your goal, it will usher in your best days. Remember, everything is working out for your good. The good, the bad, and the ugly. It's all developing you into becoming the Godly woman which you are destined to be. A true goal of a Proverbs 31 woman is to remain steadfast and unmovable, planted in her purpose. This is not the time to step out of your purpose lane. A Proverbs 31 woman is aware that her lane of purpose which she travels will ultimately lead her to her treasure in life. This is the life of fulfillment, blessings, and the life of favor with God and with man. The one who reaches this place in life is the one who's never given up despite the struggles and heartbreaks experienced throughout their journey. Metaphorically speaking, once you've received the key through your divine purpose given by God, this key will unlock stored away blessings. You might've forgotten about these particular blessings, or felt they'd never be granted to you. Now that you're walking in your purpose, you should always have an attitude of gratitude. Thanking God always for His perfect plan for your life. Remain positive no matter what because the only way is up from here. I know that you are excited, and I am excited for you. You are even closer to becoming a Proverbs 31

woman. I prophesy to you that this is your season of overflow! Each of those bad relationships and experiences are OVER. No more stagnation because you are moving forward in the right direction. God has kept you through it all so that you could see your better days! It is indeed time to live your best life, all while serving God. A lot of women fail to realize that they can in fact enjoy life as a saved individual. The fun doesn't stop, as a matter of fact it's just beginning once you receive Jesus Christ as Lord and Savior. Walking in your purpose gives you the ability to create an abundant life which God desires for you to live. That's exactly why when we're living outside of the will of God, as Christians we have many lows and very few highs. That's only because you weren't walking in your God given purpose. Walking in your purpose is simply obeying God's will for your life. This is the moment where you are about to experience the joy of the Lord! This joy is unexplainable and it feels amazing! The joy of the Lord will always be felt at its maximum level after you've discovered your divine purpose.

I am truly thankful to God that He has blessed me with the gifts that He has given me. My gifts have made room for me to enjoy my life and walk in my divine purpose. No matter what, I will always remain purpose driven. There is peace when you walk in your purpose. It's a certain level of protection that you receive. Walking in your purpose gives you the power that you need in order to empower others. This feeling is wonderful! My prayer is for you and so many other women to read this book and receive whatever it is that they need to become the Proverbs 31 woman which God desires for all of His daughters to be.

Poem

THE VIRTUOUS WOMAN
OF PROVERBS 31

P31W SHINE

A P31W is a woman of grace,
A woman of love, she's Godly and full of wonder
Every day she slays, prays,
And puts the enemy a sunder.

She leads in the right direction
A woman, a wife,
A mother full of affection
She exemplifies perfection.

Her status is secured,
She makes bread
To break bread
Her loved ones stay fed.

She rises early
And settles late
Her relationship with God is never up for debate.
In Heaven awaits her greatest estate!

She's the holder of her beauty
It reaches far beyond her skin,
In her eyes, in her heart
God gets the glory for such a beautiful work of art.
A P31W is always set apart!

She's set apart for God's glory
And for God's kingdom,

She realizes living for him
There is peace, power, deliverance and freedom.

She's as bold as a lion
And as gentle as a dove,
Her hopes are built
On things eternal and above.

Her creativity is one of a kind,
Her brilliance will always shine
She is certainly a woman
That values her time.

She's wise,
but yet humble
Never worry,
Complain, or grumble

Strong and stern, a P31W never forgets
the lessons she's learned
She's always prepared for life
And its twists and turns

A P31W stands firm
On the sword of the spirit
(Which is the word of God)
When you see one, let her know
How much she's admired, valued, and loved

Scripture: Proverbs 31:29-30
29-"Many daughters have done virtuously but you outshine
them all. 30- Charm is deceitful and beauty is vain, but
a woman who fears the Lord she shall be praised..."

Signed, A Proverbs 31 Woman <3

Chapter 6

EMBRACE THE NEW YOU

Philippians 3:13 tell us, "Forget those things which are behind us and reach forth to those things which are before…" We must understand that the first step to embracing any kind of change in life is to abandon the things of our past. Past failures, pitfalls, past misunderstandings, past relationships and so on. Those negative experiences from your past should not have any effect on where you are headed presently. The reason why most people have a difficult time embracing their new life is because they fear the unknown. People fear whatever they don't completely understand. Scripture has it in Proverbs 4:7, "In all thy getting get an understanding…" When you become a new creature in Christ, you do whatever it takes to broaden your understanding. Until you get the understanding which you need on your journey, I advise you to trust in God knowing that He will guide you every step of the way. The moment that you decide to embrace the new you, your life will then turn around completely. This new woman you're becoming will need plenty of attention. Be sure to cater to her everyday. It's important to love yourself unconditionally. As they say, "Self love is the best love!" Speaking positive affirmations over yourself daily is one way to accomplish embracing the woman you're becoming. I have a list of daily affirmations at the end of my book which you can recite daily. In order to embrace this new you, you must unapologetically accept who you're becoming. Self acceptance will take you far along your journey to becoming a Proverbs 31 woman. Accept everything about who you are. After all that you've been through and everything you've overcome, you need a change! Take a moment to think about all of the obstacles you've been faced with. Indeed, it is your season for a great change! When my season for change approached me, I was beyond ready. I was sick and tired of the same old way of living. One of the things that I've learned most is that when an individual is ready for change, there is one thing the person must be willing to work on. The quality which needs improvement, and sticks out far more than any other, would have to be their attitude. Your attitude is a strong representation of who you are. The mental state that you've settled for has been the powersource forming your entire behavior. Plus, your attitude is a behavioral attribute which demands your attention.

As a Proverbs 31 woman, the characteristics of your attitude should always mimic the fruit of the Holy Spirit. There are nine attributes which are found within the fruit of the Holy Spirit located in Galatians 5:22-23. They are as follows... love, joy, peace, longsuffering, kindness, goodness, faithfulness, meekness, and self control. When you allow the power of the Holy Spirit to transform you, then your new attitude will be evidence of this amazing transformation. Operating in the fruit of the Holy Spirit is one way Christ distinguishes his true servants. Matthew 7:16 states, "You should know them by their fruit..." God's spirit will always produce good fruit. The fruit listed in Galatians 5:22 is simply a reflection of God's character reproduced in a follower of Christ. Without this mandatory transformation, you will never reach your destination of becoming a Proverbs 31 woman.

Your attitude surely determines your altitude. Your attitude is the vehicle that not only takes you where you desire to go in life, but it also determines how far you will go in life. Your attitude will either make you or break you. As a Proverbs 31 woman, it is very important to keep your atmosphere positive. This is why it's important for you to maintain a positive attitude, for your attitude shapes your atmosphere. In order to embrace the new you, you must first leave the old you in the past. Embracing change is not as bad as it seems, especially when it involves growth. No one should desire to remain the same person all of their lives. When you're changing to grow, that means you are changing into the woman who God has ordained for you to be since the beginning of time. You must look at yourself in a mirror and tell yourself, "I love the new and improved me!" This chapter in your life story will definitely be one of the greatest. Continue to allow God to work on you. You are getting closer to becoming a Proverbs 31 woman. God handpicked you, and you were made by God in a special way. Psalm 139:14 states, "I praise You, for I am fearfully and wonderfully made. Wonderful are your works; my soul knows it very well." "You are special to God! Your capabilities are endless. Ephesians 2:10 states, "We are God's handy work created in Christ Jesus to do great works, which God prepared for us to do…" God is so amazing and we are His artwork. He created you with skill and you have a specific purpose to fulfill in life. God wants to do so much through you in this life. That is why embracing the new you is extremely important because you are allowing God's plan to go forth. His plan is the best plan for your life. Any plan outside of God's plan will fail you! Walk in your newness because there is a flood of blessings awaiting you on the other side. Your obedience will cause a shift to take place. The dry season you've been experiencing will come to a complete halt. Your obedience will usher in a waterfall of blessings. Get ready! The blessings will cascade into your life for simply positioning yourself to where you're supposed to be. God is ready to use you mightily in His kingdom. Proverbs 31 woman, your future's so BRIGHT!

Chapter 7

I was Chosen by God to be a Proverbs 31 Woman for my Husband

The first step to understanding the meaning of a Proverbs 31 woman is to observe the scripture and dissect the text. You also want to know who the audience was intended to be. As well as the actual reason that this passage was written. Now, a lot of people like to begin reading from Proverbs 31:10-31, but if you back up just a little bit to Proverbs 31:1 it informs you that this passage was actually written to a male. It was a teaching from his mother. Let's take a look at Proverbs 31:1. Scripture has it, "The words of King Lemuel an article that his mother taught him..." Now if you paid attention, you'd see that it was actually a conversation between a mother and her son. Often times, mothers like to give their children good advice. In this case, this woman wanted to advise her son of what he should look for in a wife. Once I became aware of that, I realized how I could benefit from this model given directly from the word of God. Every verse of this passage I felt was beneficial in guiding me on the road to becoming the woman I was chosen to be. Guidance is a necessary requirement when attempting to reach your destiny. Any type of guidance won't do, but the right guidance such as spiritual guidance is what you must seek. We all should have the right blueprint to follow in life. Believe it or not, the word of God is a living and true word for us to read, learn, and live by. Quite simply, it's our blueprint as believers of Christ. After I discovered how gracious God is by giving us the actual steps to becoming Godly women. I came to the conclusion as christians we are to be the right type of women for God first, second ourselves, and then our husbands. I was left in awe once discovering that it was actually a woman who was critiquing her son on what to look for in a future wife. I realized that if we had more mothers who were following this woman's example in Proverbs 31, then the divorce rate would likely be much lower. How would a man know when a good woman is in his midst if he's not correctly taught what to look for and exactly how he should treat and love his prize. So many men mistreat Godly women due to misguidance in their upbringing. Speaking from a woman's perspective, I myself had a failed marriage at a very young age. I began a seven year marriage at the age of eighteen to my first husband. After that experience, I made it up in my mind that the next time I exchange vows with someone, I was going to operate differently. I would be accepting nothing less than the best, all while being the best version of myself. I realized that I possessed everything which I needed in order to have a home filled with love and blessings. That which I seeked was already present on the inside of me. I didn't need to sit and talk to a therapist, nor did I need to envy another woman's life. Lastly, I certainly didn't need to follow the advice of another woman who also experienced a failed marriage. All I needed was a prayer life, a made up mind, and most importantly… my blueprint which is the word of God. Ladies, the word of God is all the guidance that you need in order to have a successful marriage. After carefully studying and meditating on the word of God, I knew that my next marriage would be a devine marriage orchestrated by God himself. I would know the do's, the dont's, the pros, and the cons. Of course I knew that no marriage would ever be perfect, but what I did realize was that it's possible for two people to be perfect for one another. Becoming a Proverbs 31 woman and wife became a much more reachable goal. At this point I not only had God's word to guide me, but I now had my own experience which taught me a whole lot. Ladies, I would like to encourage you to not allow the failures of life to weigh you down. Instead use everything that you go through as an inspiration to become better. That's exactly what I did and continue to do presently. I am one to learn from my mistakes and become better. It's a never ending process and you will become a better woman overall when you learn to use your past failures as a guide to becoming a better you. I came to the conclusion that I cannot become a Proverbs 31 woman to my husband unless I first become better to God as well as to myself. Think about it, how can you become a good thing to a man unless you first become a better version of yourself. The Bible states in Proverbs 18:22, "He who finds a wife finds a good thing and obtains favor from the lord..." As I meditated on that scripture, what stood out to me the most were the words "good thing". At that moment, I knew what to insert into my prayer. Paraphrase: "Lord, allow me to be my next husband's good thing." You must pray and ask God to make you over. Sometimes you have to take a moment to work on yourself, meaning to do a bit of soul searching. The first step to working on yourself is to pray for the power of God, which is already present on the inside of you, to do a perfect work in and through you. That's what you would identify as a spiritual makeover. A spiritual makeover is definitely crucial when attempting to becoming a better individual on any level. I began to pray to my father God in Heaven in the name of his son, Jesus, on a daily basis. When you begin to take your prayer life seriously, God will then honor your request. Having a prayer life is everything to me because the more you pray, the more power you'll posses. For any of my single ladies, when a man finds you he's going to see the spark in your eyes. He's going to recognize the wholeness and how complete you are even without a man. He will also witness how certain you are of yourself. He will admire your confidence all while noticing that you are already heading in the right direction. This is exactly why we as women must learn from our mistakes, otherwise we will be repeating cycles and possibly miss out on a true Godsent man. This Godsent man may simply pass you by because he doesn't see the light within you shining bright. On the other hand, he may even go out with you a time or two, but eventually he will be turned off by something you could have said or done. This turn off could very well be something as simple as a undesirable conversation, or foolish action. Those are the two ways you can actually win in the courting process. In my opinion, wise actions, along with meaningful conversations with lots of chemistry are truly the keys when desiring to win a man's heart.

A lot of women fail at a man choosing them to be his wife because they allow old ways, traits, and habits to keep them from becoming a man's good thing. You must live to learn while learning to live. Never allow your past experiences, mistakes, failures, and old behaviors to hinder you from the becoming the wife which you desire to be. Praise God because you are well on your way to becoming the Proverbs 31 woman which the Bible speaks of. I am so excited that God chose me to take this journey with you! As we continue to unlock this powerful woman who has been kept hidden on the inside of you, I want you to envision her and get a clear picture in your head of who you really are. That's right! See yourself as the woman you long to be, the woman scripture speaks of in Proverbs 31:10-31. The one thing I want you to realize from this chapter is that you can become, or be, an incredible wife no matter your past situations. All you must do is follow God's blueprint. This woman that you desire to become is not far away, she's only a prayer away. You just have to be willing to receive the better version of yourself.

It doesn't matter your age, ladies! You're never too old or too young to improve. Okay now hurry and read the final chapter! I know that you are beginning to feel brand new. Your journey to becoming a Proverbs 31 woman is soon to be accomplished!

Chapter 8

P31W, IT IS YOUR TIME TO SHINE

Congratulations! You have made it! You are ready to shine BRIGHT for Jesus Christ. It is your moment for God's glory to shine bright on you now that you have surrendered to Him. You've gotten over the most challenging phase of your journey and transition. God's glory is all over you. Your friends, family, and all others that have known you will recognize your shine. Everyone will know that it had to be the power of God which transformed you into the phenomenal woman which you have become. Scripture has it in Matthew 5:15, "Let your light shine before men that they may see your good works and glorify your Father which is in Heaven…" Allowing your light to shine has little to nothing to do with you, but it has everything to do with God. God desires for us to share his glory, as long as we return His glory back to Him. Remember, our ultimate purpose for existence in life is to bring our heavenly Father God glory, everything we do as Proverbs 31 women should edify God and His kingdom. Your behavior will either benefit God's kingdom, or work against the kingdom of God. There are so many people in this world searching for a solution and ways to get out of their mess. You will become a living testimony to those individuals who you come in contact with. They will be able witness from your transformation how God can turn trouble into triumph. Your life of victory will give them the hope which they need. It is time for you to let your light shine bright so that men can see your good works and glorify Father God in Heaven. Sometimes you have to personalize scripture and place yourself in it. I do it all the time. Doing this helps me to feel a closer connection to God. You must keep in mind that as children of God, we are the light of the world and the salt of the earth. As Christians, we add the flavor that this world is missing. Whenever you aren't shining your brightest for Jesus, somewhere along the way you have either lost your flavor or haven't discovered it yet. You must do what God has chosen you to do and allow your light to shine in this world. It's all about God's will, not yours. You must step out on faith, believe in yourself, and believe in God. You could never go wrong obeying God. A person that's living in God's will always has people wondering how they are able to shine so bright. As the Holy Spirit allows the attention to be drawn to you, your duty is to return that same attention to God. Your good works will be the thing that will capture the attention of those who's witnessing your shine. Remain faithful and humble to God always, through your love, courage, diligence, and service. In this season, you will have an unexplainable zeal for life. The radiance of God which you exemplify can never be replaced. It's time to be eager to shine for Jesus. To be eager to shine for Jesus is to simply long for the moment to help make a difference in the lives of others especially offering Christ to them. There's no gift that can compare to the gift of salvation. It's time for you to be the change that others need to see. Your life will be a life of significance. Now that you have stepped out of your comfort zone, God can use you in an impactful fashion. It's not about being in the spotlight. It's more about others spotting your light. Those who don't know you, are going to want to know who you are now, they will begin to get a little bit inquisitive. You are beginning to shine so bright people want to know what's the secret, how are you able to shine so bright. Others will begin to want the same radiance as you, but that is clearly the goal and mission. Actually, the true purpose of you shining bright is for you to gain the interest of others, in order to win them over to Christ. Remember, your light is valuable and powerful. If you aren't prayed up you can very well become fearful of this new woman you're becoming. Often times, people begin to shine so bright that they become afraid of their own light because God's glory is powerful and supernatural. Your natural mind will never be able to comprehend it all. When an individual try to grasp it from a natural place it becomes overwhelming, and that's exactly how the spirit of fear creeps in. Don't become afraid because the Spirit of God can't and won't work in you if you are operating in a spirit of a fear. Being fearful is not attractive at all. Also, You must never fear what others may say or think of you.

God can care less about the responses of others. He's more concerned about their souls! The worst thing that you can do at this point in your journey is be unsure of yourself. You must be confident, for there is power in an individual's confidence. Go to God in prayer and ask for God to grant you the confidence of Christ, and he will answer your prayer. Once you've gained the confidence that you need, you must immediately begin to walk in your calling. There will be people who won't support you, people who will hate on your progress and success. However, you must keep going. Your aim is to live a life that is pleasing to God and not to man. You must ignore the hate and continue to be great! Under no circumstances should you allow the negativity of others to cause you to step out of character. Now, this may not be easy, but it is certainly necessary. God will eventually place the right people in your life, and those individuals will both support you and help you reach your God given destiny. Because it is in fact your time to shine, you have to stay focussed. There will also be people who would rather compete with you. Some will even try to imitate your shine in hopes that they'll outshine you. Don't worry, the gift that God has given you is so authentic and original. You should never be concerned about senseless competition because when God made you he created you one of a kind. Becoming your best you on purpose is vital in this stage. Continue to follow God's path, for everything you've gone through in life is about to make sense. The pain that you had to endure was the pain that you needed to experience in order to push you to your purpose. Now that you're living your purpose, everything is beginning to feel so right and liberating. You were actually apart of a spiritual warfare as you fought to become this woman, and you won the fight! It's time to give yourself a pat on the back because this road you've been traveling wasn't an easy one, but you overcame every obstacle and broke every barrier. Scripture has it in Romans 8:37, "Know in all these things we are more than conquerors through him who loved us..." I must say myself that I appreciate where I am in my journey.

It took a lot of growth and maturity to get me where I am today. In the quest to becoming a better woman, it is essential to love and cherish yourself. I prophetically decree that your days of bitterness, self hate, isolation, anger, feeling unloved, unhappiness, having suicidal thoughts, feeling unworthy, and every bit of pain. It has all come to an end in Jesus name! A Proverbs 31 woman takes full responsibility for her actions. She admits her mistakes and is very apologetic for her wrong actions. Those who love you will love you genuinely both inside and out. It's all about becoming a living example in the kingdom of God. Becoming a better wife, mother, and overall a better woman of God should always remain apart of your motivation. You have found your voice! Think about it, you are now aware of your value and self worth. It is easier to become the woman which whom you desire to be. It is your time to represent the Proverbs 31 woman that the Bible speaks of. Now that you have found yourself, it is time to help and cultivate other women to become a Proverbs 31 woman as well. **P31W SHINE!**

Conclusion

Being able to live life as a Proverbs 31 woman is such an amazing privilege. Throughout the journey, you live, learn, and most importantly you grow. God desires for each of His daughters to shine brighter and brighter each and every day. We are the trophies of Christ in which He has won for the kingdom of God. Let's continue to make our heavenly Father God proud by allowing our light to shine! You are that wife, mother, and woman of God which you desire to be. Continue to keep your faith alive, and continue to strive. If you so happen to fall, dust yourself off and try again because God's grace is sufficient for you (2 Corinthians 12:9). Continue to take your journey one day a time, and move at your own individual pace. Never compare where you are in your journey to another Proverbs 31 woman. Like most things in life, the transformation won't happen overnight. It will continue to take effort on your behalf, a prayer life, and most importantly a committed relationship to God.

I encourage you to become apart of our dynamic, loving, powerful sisterhood to receive the spiritual, emotional, and uplifting support. You will definitely need to surround yourself with positive like-minded women. We offer weekly Bible study, prayer, impactful discussions VIA conference call, entrepreneurial opportunities, our yearly

P31W SHINE IRON SHARPENS: IRON WOMEN'S CONFERENCE,

and so much more!

It's time to be apart of something great,
so join the movement today!

Here in P31W SHINE, we have a motto which I love
for ALL of my fellow Proverbs 31 sisters to recite each
and every week before ending our conference call.
The Holy Spirit had given it to me one day during
prayer, and I would like to share it with you all...

"Just like Iron sharpens Iron, we are P31 Women
and we will FOREVER SHINE!"

31 Daily I AM Affirmations

These I AM Daily Affirmations will formulate, affirm, and work in your life!

1. I AM a new creature in Christ Jesus.
2. I AM the head and not the tail.
3. I AM above only and never beneath.
4. I AM a lender and never a borrower.
5. I AM wealthy and strong.
6. I AM whole and wise.
7. I AM healthy and God has blessed me with longevity.
8. I AM positive, prosperous, and productive in every area of my life.
9. I AM fearfully and wonderfully made.
10. I AM original and creative.
11. I AM more than enough.
12. I AM powerful and anointed.
13. I AM a loving and submissive wife.
14. I AM a wonderful, caring, and great mother.
15. I AM a doer of God's Holy word.
16. I AM a tither and seed sower.
17. I AM full of the spirit of God.
18. I AM responsible and intentional.
19. I AM honest, loving, and compassionate.
20. I AM genuine and positive.
21. I AM fruitful, and a multiplier.
22. I AM successful and secure with myself.
23. I AM courageous and confident.
24. I AM a blessing to my family, my friends, and many others.

25. I AM likable and I have the favor of God with God and with man.
26. I AM blessed and liberated.
27. I AM protected and covered by the blood of Jesus.
28. I AM beautiful and generous.
29. I AM a true servant of the God who created the Heavens and the earth.
30. I AM complete, happy, and filled with joy.
31. I AM a Proverbs 31 Woman!

"I would like to dedicate this poem to all of the women who have purchased and read my book. Thank you!"

-Dr. Tameka Trask.

Poem

P31W SHINE

P31W SHINE

Extraordinary is she
Love sits in the very
Palm of her hands
She's not a sweetheart by chance

Her presence is filled
With sparks
Which have the ability
To ignite any atmosphere

She exemplifies true elegance
Grace and class
God has given her a crown
Which will forever last

Her crown is far
From anything tangible
As a matter of fact,
It is miraculously supernatural

Her crown is not
A one size fits all
This royal piece is
Only fit for one

You are the master
Of you own crown
Place it where it belongs
And walk in your destiny!

My Prayer

Dear most gracious, almighty, wonderful God,
I thank you for enabling me to write this book. Thank
you for every female who will read this book and gain
the tools which they need to become the Godly Proverbs
31 woman that you have ordained for them to be. Lord,
I give you all the glory for all of the blessings that
you've bestowed upon me, as well as the blessings to
come. Father God, I ask that you continue to allow
my light to shine brighter than ever. I pray that you
continue to grant me the wisdom and ability to be
the wife, mother, and Visionary that you have chosen
me to be. Lord, I declare that this book will reach
and give new life to the masses. In the mighty and
miraculous name of your son Jesus Christ, Amen.

Special Thanks and Dedication

First and foremost, I would like to thank you God. I love you with all of my heart! Thank you Father for being my source, my sufficiency, and for choosing me to make an impact around the world. I know that as long as the Lord is within me, I will never fail (Psalms 46:5).

I would also like to give a special thanks to my parents for believing in me. Thank you Mom and Dad for your encouragement. Thank you for your love, support, and most importantly your prayers. I will always love and be there for the both of you.

I would like to take this opportunity to thank and dedicate my book to my wonderful and supportive husband. Baby, thank you for all that you do. You are truly an amazing husband and I love you!

Last, but certainly not least, I would like to dedicate my book and give a very special thanks to my four brilliant, amazing, daughters.

My love, my blessing, my angel, and my star! Thank you for loving me, never giving up on me, and believing in me every step of the way. Mommy wants y'all to know that you all will forever be my greatest motivation and inspiration. I will continue to be the Proverbs 31 woman before you all. May God always bless you my daughters. Forever in my heart, love Mom.

Proverbs 31:28- "Her children arise up and call her blessed. Her husband also, and he praiseth her."

About the Author

Dr. Tameka Trask is the founder and visionary of P31W SHINE women's ministry. As the leader of the ministry, she is able to cultivate women into becoming the best version of themselves while serving Jesus Christ. She has a genuine love for God and His people and is truly dedicated to serving the Lord. Dr. Tameka Trask has a true passion for preaching God's word and for writing about His greatness. Being able to lead others to Christ and seeing souls saved is her number one goal. She has been a thriving entrepreneur for decades with a drive to always pursue the next level of achievements. She resides in Houston, Texas with her loving husband and four beautiful daughters.

Contact Information

Dr. Tameka Trask Social Media Sites:
Facebook- @DrTamekaTrask
Instagram- @drtamekatrask
P31W SHINE Sites:
Website- www.P31WSHINE.com
Facebook Women's Group- P31W SHINE
Iron Sharpens Iron Women's Group
Instagram- @p31wshine
Twitter- @P31WSHINE
Follow us on all of our social media sites for inquiries and information about future events! Join our P31W SHINE Iron Sharpens Iron Women's Group on Facebook to interact with our uplifting group of Proverbs 31 Women!

Printed in the United States
By Bookmasters